Journey Through
FRANCE

LIZ GOGERLY
&
ROB HUNT

W
FRANKLIN WATTS
LONDON•SYDNEY

Franklin Watts

Published in Great Britain in 2017 by The Watts Publishing Group

Credits

Editor in Chief: John Miles

Series Editor: Amy Stephenson

Series Designer: Emma DeBanks

Picture Researcher: Diana Morris

Picture Credits: Adeliepenguin/Dreamstime: 3, 9t, 14b. Alexandrpeers/Dreamstime: 7bra. Jelena Aloskina/Dreamstime: 16b. Annemario/ Dreamstime: 8b. Aristos/Dreamstime: 29t. Artushfoto/Dreamstime: 9bl. Atlas Photo Archive/Topfoto: 28c. Authors Image Ltd/Alamy: 22. Jay Beiler/Dreamstime: 18. Barbara Broker Boensch /Image Broker /Robert Harding PL: 25tr. Sebastien Bonaimé/Dreamstime: 6bl. Gunold Brunbauer/ Dreamstime: 15t. Brunohlaver/Dreamstime: 6cr. Neil Burton/Dreamstime: 15b. Ysbrand Cosijn /Shutterstock: 23b. Eduardo Gonzalez Diaz/ Dreamstime: 7tr, 27c. Pavel Dospiva/Dreamstime: 12b. Pierre Jean Durieu/Dreamstime: 16c. Max Earey/Shutterstock: 25b. Soren Egeberg/ Dreamstime: 5b. Mary Evans PL/Alamy: 5t. Heike Falkenberg/Dreamstime: 7tc. Ed Francissen/Dreamstime: 1, 10b. Radu Razvan Gheorghe/ Dreamstime: 13b. Zheng Huang/Shutterstock: 26b. Andrei Iancu /Dreamstime: 6cla, 15c. Olga Itina/Dreamstime: 7bl. Oleg Ivanov/Dreamstime: 6cl, 20. Ixuskmitl/Dreamstime: 8t. Michael Jenner/Robert Harding PL: 25tl. Juliann/Shutterstock: 6tl. Konstantin/Dreamstime: front cover. Veniamin Kraskov/Dreamstime: 19t, 19b. Ivan Kravtsov/Dreamstime: 7cr. Julie Kuznetsova/Dreamstime: 13t. Ldambies/Dreamstime: 21t. Giancarlo Liguori/ Dreamstime: 4. Lunamarina/Dreamstime: 7bc. Daniela Manginca/Dreamstime: 11c. Pedro Nantes: 24t. Joris van Ostaeyen/Dreamstime: 27t. Ekaterina Pokrovsky/Dreamstime: 11t. Ganna Poltoratska/Dreamstime: 7c. Prostogugs/Dreamstime: 21br. RG-V/Shutterstock: 10c. Richard Semik/Dreamstime: 6c.Vitaly Titov & Maria Sideinkova/Dreamstime: 23c. SiefkinDR /NMA, Saint-Germain-en-Laye/CC Wikimedia: 17t. Sivitri /Dreamstime: 7br. Anton Sokolov/Dreamstime: 7tl. Sonechka/Dreamstime: 12c. Olga Vasileva/Dreamstime: 27b. verslecentre.com: 17c. Thierry Vialard/Dreamstime: 23t. Ints Vikmanis/Dreamstime: 7tcl. Vvoevale/Dreamstime: 24b. Ivonne Wierink/Shutterstock: 28-29b. CC Wikimedia: 11b, 21bl. Yarchyk /Dreamstime: 17b. Huang Zheng/Shutterstock: 9br. Ziye/Dreamstime: 26t.

Dewey number: 944

ISBN: 978 1 4451 3661 5

Printed in Malaysia

Franklin Watts

An imprint of

Hachette Children's Group

Part of The Watts Publishing Group

Carmelite House

50 Victoria Embankment

London EC4Y 0DZ

An Hachette UK Company

www.hachette.co.uk

www.franklinwatts.co.uk

CONTENTS

VIVE LA FRANCE!

France, with a total land area of approximately 550,000 km², is the biggest country in western Europe and home to a wide variety of people, languages, climates and geographical features. It might be big, but it is easy to get around because it has a great transport system. If you're up very early, you can have a quick breakfast of croissants in the north of France, zip to the Alps by lunchtime for a snappy ski session and then finish off by briefly basking in the evening sun on a beach in the south!

▼ You can enjoy sunshine all year round at the resort of Nice in the south of France.

A rich history

France has been inhabited by humans for over 1.8 million years. These prehistoric people painted some of the earliest surviving pictures of animals on the walls of their caves. Over the centuries, France has survived countless wars and a couple of revolutions to become one of the most successful and influential countries on Earth.

The French language

The official language of France is French but around the country there is a wide variety of languages and dialects spoken, including Alsatian, Basque, Breton and Walloon.

► The Montgolfier brothers made the first manned balloon flight in 1783.

French firsts in transport

The French were the first to suggest a tunnel under the English Channel; they were the first to fly in balloons (see right); and Frenchman Louis Blériot was the first to fly a winged aircraft across the English Channel in 1909. In 1969 the French helped build the first passenger plane capable of supersonic flight – Concorde.

French people may speak many different languages but the citizens of France are very protective about their official language. They do not want French to become diluted by English and Americanisms and have set up a website so people can suggest suitable French alternatives to new English words like 'tweet' or 'hashtag'. Thanks to this, French people no longer have to download a podcast and send it in an email – they can *télécharger une baladodiffusion* and send it in *un courriel*.

Sunshine and snow

France has a varied geography and four very different climates. On any one day, as trees are being bent over by the Mistral wind in Provence, someone can be getting a suntan on the Côte d'Azur, while someone else is wiping icicles off their nose in the Pyrénées.

▲ A skier zips through the powdery snow high up on a French mountain.

JOURNEY PLANNER

YOUR JOURNEY

English Channel

Cherbourg

Le Hav

Bayeux

Mont Saint-Michel   Saint-Lô   Cae

5

Brest

Alenç

Saint-Brieuc

Quimper   Laval

Lorient   Rennes ◎

Vannes

1

Angers

Saint-Nazaire

Belle-Île   **Nantes**

La Roche-sur-Yor

Île d'Yeu

2   **3**

Île de Ré   Nior

La Rochelle

Île d'Oléron

Angoulê

4

Bor

Mont-de-Marsa

Bay of Biscay

Biarritz

Orthez   Pa

KEY

— your route around France

------- flight

— river

— road

★ capital city

4

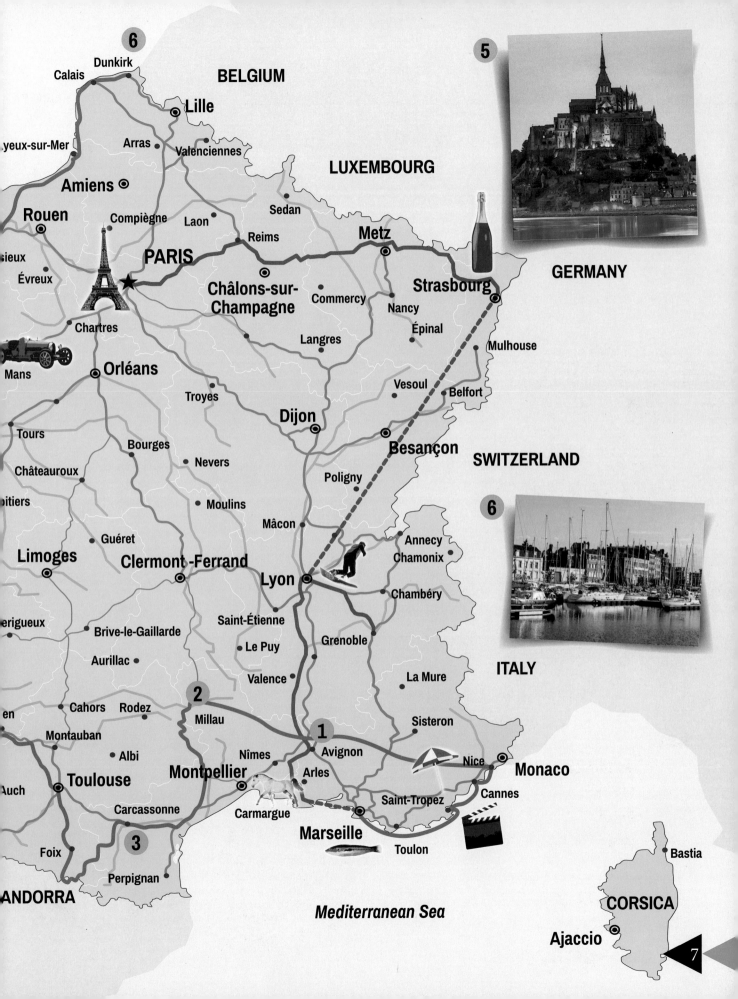

6

Dunkirk

Calais

BELGIUM

Lille

Arras

Valenciennes

yeux-sur-Mer

Amiens

LUXEMBOURG

Rouen

Compiègne

Laon

Sedan

Metz

sieux

Évreux

PARIS

Reims

Commercy

Nancy

Strasbourg

GERMANY

Chartres

Châlons-sur-Champagne

Épinal

Mulhouse

Mans

Orléans

Troyes

Langres

Vesoul

Belfort

Tours

Bourges

Dijon

Besançon

SWITZERLAND

Châteauroux

Nevers

Poligny

itiers

Moulins

Guéret

Mâcon

Annecy

Limoges

Clermont -Ferrand

Lyon

Chamonix

6

erigueux

Brive-le-Gaillarde

Saint-Étienne

Chambéry

Aurillac

Le Puy

Grenoble

Valence

La Mure

ITALY

2

Cahors

Rodez

Millau

Sisteron

en

Montauban

Nîmes

Avignon

1

Albi

Montpellier

Arles

Nice

Monaco

Auch

Toulouse

Saint-Tropez

Cannes

Carcassonne

Carmargue

3

Marseille

Toulon

Foix

Bastia

Perpignan

ANDORRA

Mediterranean Sea

CORSICA

Ajaccio

7

PARIS

You will start your journey in France's capital, Paris. It is known as the 'city of love' or the 'city of lights' to visitors, but as Paname to many of its 2.25 million inhabitants. No one is totally sure where the name Paname comes from but it may be because of the fashion for Panama hats worn in Paris at the start of the 20th century. Today Paris is a city famous for its fashion, culture and fabulous architecture.

▼ The Eiffel Tower is a symbol of France's industrial strength and history.

Eiffel Tower

The most visible and recognisable landmark in France is probably the Eiffel Tower. It was named after the engineer who designed it, Gustave Eiffel (1832–1923), and erected for the 1889 World's Fair. It took a while before the people of Paris fell in love with it. Some never did, including the writer Guy de Maupassant (1850–1893). He hated the tower so much that it is said he insisted on eating lunch every day in the tower's restaurant, as that was the only place where he couldn't see it!

◀ One way to see Notre-Dame Cathedral is from a boat on the River Seine.

A centre for tourism

With 45 million visitors a year, Paris is one of the most visited cities in the world. The city's most visited attractions are:

1. Disneyland Paris (15 million)
2. Notre-Dame Cathedral (13.6 million)
3. Sacré-Cœur (10.5 million)
4. The Louvre (8.2 million)
5. The Eiffel Tower (6.7 million)

Getting around the city

A boat trip down the River Seine is the perfect way to see the famous landmarks without getting caught up in traffic, or you could cross it on one of the city's 37 bridges. The Pont Alexandre III was completed in 1900. With its gilded statues and ornate lamp posts, it is one of the most beautiful bridges in the world.

Another way to whizz around this city is on its vast underground train system called the Paris Métro. Some parts of the system date back to the early 20th century and have a distinct Art Nouveau style. Paris is great for cyclists too and you can hire bicycles easily and cheaply from one of 1,230 bicycle stations.

Parisian chic

However you choose to get about, you will probably notice that many people here know how to dress well – they are 'chic', which means they are stylish. Parisians are famous for their smart clothes and the city is a major centre for fashion. World-renowned 20th-century designers based in Paris include Coco Chanel, Pierre Cardin and Christian Dior. Without Paris we wouldn't have the little black dress, *haute couture*, modern bras, polo shirts or bikinis.

▼ Parisians love fashion and take pride in wearing chic clothes.

▼ Bicycles for hire on a Parisian street.

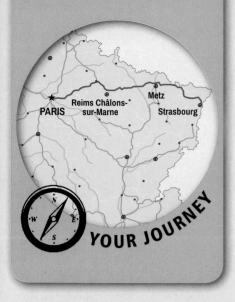

YOUR JOURNEY

PARIS TO STRASBOURG

It's time to jump in a car, say farewell to Paris, and travel east to Strasbourg. The most appropriate car to drive has to be a Bugatti sports car because, although Bugatti is an Italian name, the company is based in the Alsace town of Molsheim, which is about 30 km from Strasbourg.

Real Champagne

Strasbourg is the capital city of the Alsace region. On your way to Strasbourg you will pass through the Champagne region. Remember to take note of the vineyards that you pass through. These grow some of the most notable grapes in the world, used to make the sparkling white wine called Champagne. There are many other types of sparkling wine produced around the world but only the wines from this area can be called Champagne.

▼ A popping Champagne cork can reach a speed of around 50 mph as it leaves the bottle.

Local languages

When you arrive in Strasbourg you will be struck by its architecture and historic feel. Medieval and Gothic buildings give the city a truly fairytale feeling. One of the best ways to soak up the city's magical atmosphere is by taking a boat trip on the canal. Do not be surprised to hear Alsatian being spoken in many places – this is a regional dialect, more related to German than French. Alsatian is declining in use and lots of Strasbourgers speak French or German. This is because Strasbourg is near the German border, and several times in its history the area has been claimed as part of Germany.

▲ Listen out for people speaking French, German and Alsatian on the streets of Strasbourg.

European Parliament

Strasbourg is the official seat of the European Parliament. The Parliament meets here twelve times a year to make new laws, make sure all its member states are behaving democratically, and decide how money will be spent in the European Union.

◄ The distinctive round tower of the European Parliament building in Strasbourg.

Louis Pasteur

Louis Pasteur (1822–1895) was a scientist whose research work saved millions of lives. He was a professor at the University of Strasbourg. He discovered vaccines for rabies and anthrax and paved the way for cures for deadly diseases such as cholera, malaria and tuberculosis. He also found a way to preserve milk, wine and cheese. The process was named after him and is called pasteurisation. He's so important, that for many years, the city honoured him by calling the University's science faculty *Université Louis-Pasteur*. Later it was absorbed by the rest of the University of Strasbourg, but his legacy lives on around the world.

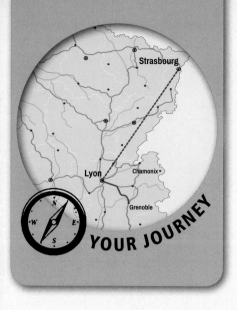

YOUR JOURNEY

STRASBOURG TO THE ALPS

Strasbourg has its own airport and it's from here that you will catch a flight to your next destination – the Alps. You will land in Lyon, known as the gateway to the Alps, and transfer to 'the capital of the Alps', Grenoble, on a ski-shuttle bus.

An almighty crash

The enormous mountain range called the Alps passes through eight European countries and covers 1,200 km. These majestic mountains have been a long time in the making and are basically the result of two tectonic plates crashing together. The rocks that have risen up to create the peaks were once deep under the sea. It is quite possible that you could find fossils of sea creatures from 230 million years ago while climbing the mountains. The highest peak in the French Alps is Mont Blanc, near the French and Italian border, and it rises 4,808 m into the sky. It's the highest mountain in Europe and climbers celebrate when they reach its summit.

▲ A climber on the summit of Mont Blanc. Its name means 'white mountain'.

▼ Skiers enjoy a view of Mont Blanc from the piste.

The Mont Blanc tramway, packed with tourists.

Holiday heaven

Tourism is important to the French economy and the Alps are a beautiful place to visit throughout the year. Head to Grenoble and there are plenty of minibuses that will take you into the mountains. In the summer months hikers enjoy the beautiful scenery and swim in the warm lakes. Adventure holidays with white water rafting and bungee jumping are very popular. Later in the year the Alps become a winter wonderland for skiers and snowboarders. The French ski resorts are among the most expensive in Europe, but they are always busy because there are slopes for all levels. Courchevel is great for beginners while Val d'Isère can challenge any pro!

▶ French cyclist Pierre Rolland wearing the polka dot jersey.

Mountain railways

Passengers can sit back and relax when they board the Mont Blanc Tramway. Departing from Saint-Gervais-les-Bains, the train slowly makes its way up to Nid d'Aigle (the Eagle's Nest), which lies at 2,380 m, making it the highest railway in France. The Montenvers train at Chamonix is another winner. This train climbs 1,913 m to the bottom of the Mer de Glace – the longest glacier in France. A warm drink on the terrace of the Grand Hôtel du Montenvers and a tour of the Ice Cave in the centre of the glacier are both a must!

The 'King of the Mountains'

One of the world's most famous sporting events is the Tour de France. The cycle race route around the country varies from year to year, but it always has a stage in the Alps. The cyclist who performs best over the peaks is called the 'King of the Mountains' and wears a white top with red polka dots.

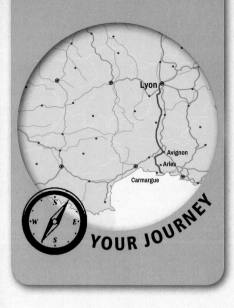

YOUR JOURNEY

LYON AND THE RHÔNE

There's a rail link from Saint-Gervais-les-Bains back to Lyon, so you can sit back and take in the mountain scenery. Lyon is the capital of the Rhône/Alps region and famous for its fine food. From there you can take a boat down the River Rhône and see some beautiful sights along the way.

Funny food

Lyon is a great place to be if you are hungry as it is considered the capital of gastronomy in France. You would have to be very brave to try *andouillette à la Lyonnaise* – it's a sausage made from pigs' intestines and it is actually meant to smell a bit like a toilet! You might be better off sticking to a traditional dish of chicken in wine – coq au vin! Lyon is also famous for its important role in the birth of cinema. It is where Auguste (1862–1954) and Louis (1864–1948) Lumière, two French brothers, made the first-ever projected film, *Workers Leaving the Lumière Factory in Lyon,* in 1895.

A powerful river

Lyon is also the place to find a river boat to take you down the River Rhône. The Rhône rises from a glacier in the Swiss Alps and flows over 800 km to the Mediterranean. You will travel along the last 310 km and you will pass 18 hydro-electric plants and pass through 12 river locks. The hydro-electric plants create clean, renewable energy (3 per cent of France's overall usage) and the locks help make the fast-flowing river easier to navigate.

▼ Lyon is the biggest industrial French city on the River Rhône.

▶ The Palace of the Popes in Avignon is Europe's largest Gothic palace.

En route for Avignon

There are many beautiful cities and towns to visit on your river cruise, including Vienne, Montélimar (where you can sample the world-famous nougat) and Viviers. You will pass through the Rhône Valley, one of the most famous wine-growing areas and where a well-known wine called Châteauneuf-du-Pape is produced. Your boat trip finishes in the historic city of Avignon. The city is famous because seven popes lived here during the 14th century. It is also the home of the famous medieval Pont d'Avignon – a collapsed bridge that only crosses part of the Rhône but looks spectacular all the same.

▶ Don't fall off the end of the Pont d'Avignon!

◀ Wild Camargue horses.

The Camargue

If you love wildlife then break your journey for a few days in the Camargue. This area of national park stretches from below Arles to the coast and it is where the Rhône divides into two. This river delta is the largest in western Europe and home to rare birdlife (including flamingoes) and flowers and plants, as well as wild bulls and the famous, white Camargue horses.

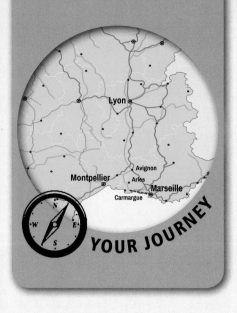

YOUR JOURNEY

MARSEILLE ON THE MED

At the end of your leisurely cruise down the Rhône, is Port-Saint-Louis-du-Rhône. From here you can catch a shuttle bus to France's second biggest city and one of the most important Mediterranean ports – Marseille.

A famous port

Marseille has a Mediterranean climate, which means it has warm, dry summers and mild, humid winters. Its geographical position makes it an ideal port and it is one of the busiest on the Mediterranean, shifting nearly 86,000 tonnes of cargo every year. The port is a major source of jobs for people who live in the area. The city's other major industries are fishing and tourism.

▲ Fishermen with their boats inside Marseille's Old Port.

◀ Traditional Marseille bouillabaisse is made with many types of fish, including the European conger eel!

Bouillabaisse

It is said that the French fish stew, known as *bouillabaisse*, was invented by the fishermen of Marseille who threw all the bony fish that they could not sell in the markets into a cooking pot with some herbs and served it to their families. It tastes better than it sounds! Make sure you try a bowlful before you depart.

An ancient city

Marseille is one of the oldest cities in western Europe. It was founded by the Greeks over 2,500 years ago and was originally called *Masallia*. Even before then, people had lived in the area for over 30,000 years! We know this because of the many prehistoric cave paintings in the area.

◄ One of the many prehistoric cave paintings found in the Cosquer cave near Marseille.

Modern housing

Le Corbusier was possibly the most influential architect of the 20th century. His great ambition was to solve the problem of overcrowding in cities. His idea was to build upwards and create 'streets in the sky'. His first attempt was the *Cité Radieuse* (Radiant City – see right) built in 1947 in Marseille. The 12-storey building, built on pillars, has a restaurant, a paddling pool, a roof-top garden, a hotel and lots of other shared facilities. It was considered a success and the ideas were copied in many other countries.

▲ A view of Chateau d'If and the Mediterranean from Marseille. The small castle on the island was once a military fortress and a prison.

The French national anthem

The French national anthem is known as *La Marseillaise* – The song of Marseille. In 1792 a group of people from Marseille sang it as they marched to Paris to join the French Revolution. It was officially adopted as the French national anthem in 1795.

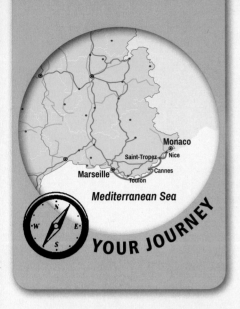
YOUR JOURNEY

CÔTE D'AZUR, THE FRENCH RIVIERA

Now it is time to travel in style and take a yacht to the French Riviera. The French refer to this part of the world as the Côte d'Azur – 'the blue coast' – because of the deep colour of the sea that laps upon the golden beaches.

Saint-Tropez

Our first stop is the famous port of Saint-Tropez. This fashionable tourist resort started out as a fishing village but during the last hundred years it has transformed into a centre of tourism for the rich and famous.

▼ Luxury yachts anchored in the sparkling blue waters off the coast of Saint-Tropez.

Cannes

The city of Cannes is about an hour away by boat from Saint-Tropez. If you're travelling during May, you might catch the Cannes Film Festival. This is where the world's film-makers meet to show and sell their movies. The top films compete for the prestigious *Palme d'Or* (the Golden Palm) and for a fortnight the town is filled with film stars partying and promoting their work.

Perfume capital of the world

Slightly inland from Cannes and a short bus-ride away is Grasse, the perfume capital of the world. Today, it produces 10 per cent of the world's supply, but it wasn't always such a sweet-smelling place! In earlier times it specialised in preparing leather. Back then, the best way to preserve leather, and make it soft enough to use, was to treat it with a mixture of urine, brains and dung! Needless to say this led to very smelly leather and an even smellier town. Rich people loved the gloves from Grasse but hated the smell, so one day someone decided to add perfume to the finished product. The result was so successful that Grasse eventually began to make perfume instead.

◀ See how perfume is made and then buy a bottle at the Fragonard perfume factory and museum in Grasse.

Nice

Hop back on a bus for the next and final stop on the Côte d'Azur, the sunny city of Nice. Not only is Nice the capital of the Côte d'Azur but it is the second most popular city for tourism in France after Paris. While you are there be sure to stroll along the Promenade des Anglais (walk of the English), a long walkway that separates the town from the beach. It takes its name from the walking habits of the wealthy English people who liked to take holidays in Nice in the early 19th century.

Art and the Riviera

The Côte d'Azur has always attracted many artists who love the light and the colours reflected off the sea. Artists such as Picasso (1881–1973), Matisse (1869–1954), Renoir (1841–1919) and Monet (1840–1926) have all lived and worked here at some point.

▶ Local people call the Promenade des Anglais, 'La Prom'.

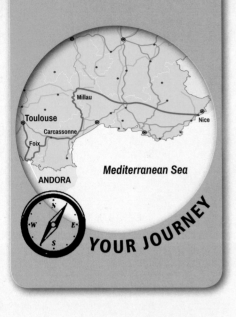

Toulouse
Millau
Carcassonne
Foix
Nice
Mediterranean Sea
ANDORA

N W E S

YOUR JOURNEY

SOUTH-WEST FRANCE

Pack away your beach clothes and hire a car at Nice because you're off to Toulouse. Along the way you'll see one of the miracles of modern architecture, visit a medieval marvel and breathe in the fresh mountain air.

A bridge in the clouds

The Millau Viaduct over the River Tarn is absolutely breathtaking. It's well worth making a detour to see this wonder of engineering, designed by the British architect Sir Norman Foster and French architect Michel Virloguex. Opened in 2004, it is the tallest bridge in the world. Its tallest mast is 343 m – which is 42 m higher than the Eiffel Tower. On cloudy days it sometimes looks like the bridge is floating on the mist.

Carcassonne

Carcassonne is a city so beautiful and interesting that UNESCO made it a World Heritage Site. Its most notable feature is the citadel – a medieval city on a hillside protected by a 3 km double wall. Make sure you stroll along the castle walls and enjoy the views of the Languedoc countryside from each of the 53 towers. One of the towers hosts the gruesome Musée de la Torture where you can see the horrible ways people were punished in the past.

▼ The Millau Viaduct is so tall clouds can form underneath the roadway!

▶ You'll be lucky to spot a Eurasian brown bear; there are only about fifteen of them living in the Pyrénées.

Road trip into the mountains

All the roads out of Carcassonne lead to areas of outstanding beauty. To the east is the Massif Central. To the west are the foothills of the Pyrénées. The steep, windy roads through the mountains are a little scary but the views are spectacular. The brown bears that used to live in these mountains were hunted out of the region by farmers. Bears have been reintroduced, but there are still fierce arguments between local sheep farmers, scared that the bears will attack their flocks, and those that want the bears to remain in the region.

Toulouse

Continue on your journey to Toulouse. This pretty city is also known as 'the Pink City' because of the extensive use of pink terracotta bricks. The other thing you may notice is that many street names are written in French and in Occitan, the local language.

▲ The sign on top is in French and the one below is in Occitan.

Andorra

Tucked away in the mountains is the tiny country of Andorra. Although it is a country in its own right, due to an historical agreement, the President of France rules the country along with the Spanish Bishop of Urgell.

▲ Andorra has a population of only 85,000 people.

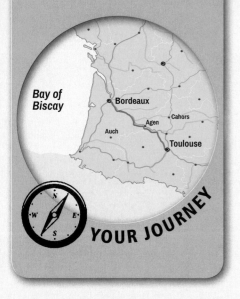

Bay of Biscay

Bordeaux

Agen Cahors

Auch

Toulouse

BARGE TO BORDEAUX

It's really quick and easy to get to Bordeaux from Toulouse by plane or train. If you have a week to make the journey, there's a cycle route along the Canal de Garonne. But, if you like things even more slow and leisurely, then travelling by barge is best.

Canal de Garonne

The River Garonne flows between Toulouse and Bordeaux but it isn't always possible to navigate all the way. The Canal de Garonne, which runs parallel to the river, was built in the 19th century for transporting goods. These days you're more likely to see tourists in barges navigating the waterway than boats carrying cargo.

▶ Canal boats moored on the Canal de Garonne.

▶ These bronze statues are part of a stunning fountain in the Place des Quinconces.

The Pearl of Aquitaine

As you may have realised by now, most French cities have nicknames and Bordeaux is no exception – in fact it has two! It used to be known as *La Belle Endormie* (Sleeping Beauty) because although it was beautiful and historic, it was also rundown and neglected. Now it has been restored to its original 18th-century glory and rejoices in the name *La perle d'Aquitaine* (The Pearl of Aquitaine). In France, only Paris has more historic buildings than Bordeaux. It has one of the biggest and most well-preserved areas of 18th-century buildings making it the perfect location for TV and film makers when they are working on historical dramas. The Place des Quinconces, built in 1820, is one of the largest city squares in Europe.

Wine capital of the world

Bordeaux is the oldest vineyard region in France and produces a wine that is arguably more famous than the city itself. Wine has been made in the area since the Romans introduced it in the 1st century and it is now the largest producer in France. Its success is down to many factors including an abundance of water from the rivers Garonne and Dordogne and the Gironde Estuary. It has a temperate climate with a high degree of humidity because of its position near the Atlantic Ocean. Every other year, Bordeaux is host to Vinexpo, the world's most important wine fair.

Big-headed dog

The Dogue de Bordeaux is a very old breed of dog that was developed in the region. It was deliberately bred to have a massive skull and jaws so that it could fight bulls, bears and boars. It was also used as a guard dog by the rich and powerful.

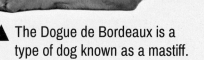

▲ The Dogue de Bordeaux is a type of dog known as a mastiff.

▲ Bordeaux wines are popular in France.

Le Mans

Nantes

Bay of
Biscay

Poitiers

Bordeaux

NANTES AND LE MANS

You can board one of France's superb TGVs to travel up the west coast of France and visit the environmentally-friendly city of Nantes. TGV stands for *train à grande vitesse* and these high-speed trains can travel at average speeds of nearly 280 mph. Afterwards, you can zoom to the ultimate city for speedsters, Le Mans.

▲ Houses at Trentemoult in Nantes, along the south bank of the Loire.

▼ A tram on one of the three tram lines in Nantes.

How green is my city?

Nantes is situated on the Loire, the longest river completely in France. If you want to see a city that is updating its transport policy to become more green then this is the place for you. In 2013 Nantes was given the European Green Capital Award because of its attempts to control the city's pollution emissions and its commitment to protecting natural spaces. It has an innovative public transport system, with one of the busiest and best electric tramways in Europe. While you're here, why don't you hire a bike so that you really blend in with the locals!

▲ Shoppers browsing at Nantes' flea market.

Market day

A visit to a French market, whether for fresh produce or interesting antiques, is one of the best ways to get to know and understand the French people. Markets take place in France in each and every village, town and city on a regular basis and Nantes has dozens to choose from every day. There is a lovely art and craft market at the ancient fishing village of Trentemoult. It's just a short boat ride away from Nantes and well worth a visit because of its trendy, bohemian atmosphere. It's a great place to stroll around and enjoy the brightly coloured houses and artistic sculptures, mosaics and wall paintings.

Le Mans

Once you've satisfied yourself with the eco-environment of Nantes, it's time to burn some rubber in a Peugeot sports car and travel to the motor city of Le Mans. A Peugeot is a suitable choice as they were the last French company to win the prestigious 24-hour Le Mans sports car race. Each year part of Le Mans is transformed into a race track as drivers test themselves and their cars in one of the oldest motor racing competitions. Much of Le Mans' economy is linked to the motor industry.

Jules Verne

Nantes is the birthplace of Jules Verne, one of France's most beloved authors. He is known as one of the 'fathers of science fiction' and wrote classics such as *20,000 Leagues Under the Sea*, *Journey to the Centre of the Earth* and, the perfect book for travellers, *Around the World in 80 Days*. Visit the Jules Verne Museum in the city.

▶ Statue of Jules Verne looking through a sextant.

▼ The last French car to win at Le Mans was this Peugeot in 2009.

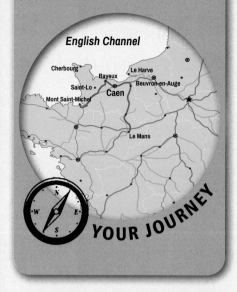

English Channel

Cherbourg
Le Harve
Bayeux
Saint-Lo · Beuvron-en-Auge
Caen
Mont Saint-Michel

Le Mans

YOUR JOURNEY

CAMPERVAN TO CAEN AND BEYOND

▼ Visitors can wander around the ramparts of the Château de Caen.

After all that zooming around in Le Mans, a change of pace is called for. You will travel on to Caen in a campervan so that you can explore Normandy in the north.

Caen's conqueror

Caen was nearly bombed to bits in the Second World War when 80 per cent of the city was destroyed. Luckily, its impressive castle, the Château de Caen, still reigns over its skyline. The castle was built by William, Duke of Normandy, in 1060. Six years later in 1066 he invaded Britain to become King William the Conqueror. It is one of the largest castles in western Europe and has been involved in many conflicts. In the Second World War it was damaged by bombs because it was used as soldiers' barracks by the Nazis.

The prettiest village in France

Half an hour outside Caen is one of the prettiest villages in France: Beuvron-en-Auge. It's well worth the journey for an overnight stay. It's a little like stepping onto a 16th-century film set, as many of the houses are multi-coloured and half-timbered. Be sure to check out the little church that is typical of the Normandy region.

▲ Half-timbered houses surround the beautiful town square of Beuvron-en-Auge.

Bayeux Tapestry or embroidery?

While you're in the area, you should make an excursion to see the Bayeux Tapestry, which is on display in Bayeux, a town west of Caen. The Bayeux Tapestry is not actually a tapestry. It is a piece of embroidered cloth, which is nearly 70 m long and tells the story of William the Conqueror's invasion of England. Studies of the dyes used in the embroidery wool suggest it was actually made in England.

▲ This section of the tapestry is believed to show William's soldiers and horses landing in Britain.

▼ The island that Mont Saint-Michel sits on is only 600 m from the mainland.

Mont Saint-Michel

Enjoy the final night in your campervan on the north-west coast. Keep heading west towards the magnificent Mont Saint-Michel. Founded as a monastery in the 8th century, it is a group of buildings on a cone-shaped rock that rises up, in fairytale fashion, from the sea. There is a bridge to drive across now, but in the past you had to navigate dangerous quicksand to get to the mount. It is now a permanent home to fewer than 50 people, but it still gets crowded as every year around 3 million tourists visit, keen to take in the magical atmosphere.

Local delicacies

On your travels make sure you taste some freshly-baked brioche because this is where they were originally made. Apples are everywhere so tuck into Norman Tart (see right), a delicious apple tart. You'll find locally-produced apple cider and calvados (apple brandy) on the menu, too.

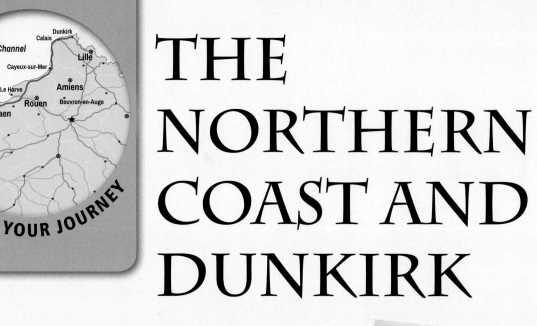

THE NORTHERN COAST AND DUNKIRK

The next part of your tour will take you by bike and steam train through a region steeped in the history of the Second World War and the D-Day Landings.

D-Day beaches

Your journey from Mont Saint-Michel to the Normandy beaches by bike may be difficult in places but it is nothing compared to the journey faced by Allied forces from Britain, the United States of America and Canada on 6 June 1944. It was that day that they set sail from England and prepared to invade German-occupied France. They faced bombs and bullets as they struggled to land and progress inland to defeat the German army and end the Second World War. Sadly, there are countless war cemeteries, memorials and museums along this stretch of coast – a testament to the huge loss of life in the pursuit of freedom.

▲ Soldiers leaving a landing craft on D-Day.

▼ Seaside towns along the Normandy coast look out onto the English Channel, known as *la Manche* (the sleeve) in France.

The five beaches where the Allies landed are along the coast between the mouth of the River Orne and and the Dunes de Varreville. These beaches have French names but they are mostly known by the code names they were given by the Allies. All the beaches are signposted and from east to west are called Sword, Juno, Gold, Omaha and Utah. Look out for a few clues to the fighting, such as the marks left by German shells and bunkers on the cliffs at Omaha. At Arromanches you can see the remains of a Mulberry harbour, used by the Allied troops to get supplies and equipment onto the beaches.

▲ The remains of a Mulberry harbour – a temporary harbour used by the British.

Le petit train de la Baie de Somme

Load your bikes onto a steam train at the lovely seaside town of Cayeux-sur-Mer, and relax as you enjoy the scenery on *le petit train de la Baie de Somme*, a heritage railway that takes you to Le Crotoy, a seaside town on the northern coast that actually faces south! Sit for a while and watch the seabirds and the seals battle for fish in the bay.

End of the road

Time to get back on your bike and enjoy the last part of your journey. You're off to Dunkirk, the most northerly town in France, which lies about 10 km from the Belgian border. Dunkirk is famous for being the departure point for the British Expeditionary Force as they fled from the German army in 1940. Local museums tell the story of that time long ago. These days the war is a distant memory and the local beaches are filled with holiday makers in the summer. Children play in the sand dunes and swimmers and surfers head into the waves. It's the perfect place for you to relax and reflect upon your amazing journey through France.

GLOSSARY

Allies
In the Second World War, the Allies were the countries that formed a coalition to oppose Germany, Italy and Japan. The Allies included Britain, the US and the USSR (the Soviet Union).

architecture
The art of designing, planning and constructing a building or structure.

bohemian
A free spirit, or a person that is socially unconventional. Often used to describe nonconformist artists and performers.

brioche
A light, sweet bread usually shaped into small rolls which is regularly eaten at breakfast in France.

croissant
A flaky, buttery pastry that is often enjoyed at breakfast in France.

Dunkirk
A town in northern France, known for being the place where more than 330,000 Allied troops were trapped by the advancing German army during the Second World War. British Prime Minister, Winston Churchill, called the Dunkirk evacuation a 'miracle'.

emissions
Particles that are given out.

European Parliament
The European Parliament was created in 1962 and members were chosen from national parliaments. These days elections are held across the EU's 28 member states every five years to choose the 751 Members of the European Parliament (MEPs).

European Union
A group of European countries that have formed an economical and political union to operate as one unit in the world economy. Created in 1993, member states include Austria, Belgium, Bulgaria, Cyprus, the Czech Republic, Denmark, Estonia, Finland, France, Germany, Greece, Hungary, Ireland, Italy, Latvia, Lithuania, Luxembourg, Malta, the Netherlands, Poland, Portugal, Romania, Slovakia, Slovenia, Spain, Sweden and the UK.

gastronomy
The art of good food.

glacier
A large mass of ice that moves down a slope.

half-timbered
Buildings made with exposed wooden frames, filled with bricks or other materials.

humidity
The amount of water in the air.

hydro-electric plants
Places that convert the energy from moving water to electricity.

inhabitants
People who live in a place.

landmark
An important feature or place in a geographical area.

medieval
The period also known as the middle ages – 500 to 1500 CE.

Mediterranean climate
An area of the planet (not necessarily near the Mediterranean Sea) that has hot, dry summers and cool, wet winters.

metropolis
A large, busy city or urban area.

monastery
A place where monks live, work and pray.

Mulberry harbour
A temporary, portable harbour used to unload goods and weapons by the British in the Second World War.

navigate
To direct a boat or an aeroplane successfully.

navigable
A part of a waterway that it is possible to navigate/ travel down.

pollution
Poisonous materials in the environment.

river delta
The flat area where a river spreads out as it meets the sea.

sextant
An instrument used by navigators for measuring the angle between two objects, such as a star and the horizon.

supersonic flight
Flying faster than the speed of sound.

tectonic plates
The plates that make up the solid outer layer of the planet. They change position very slowly and this movement can create changes in the earth. Some of these changes happen quite quickly, like earthquakes, others happen over millions of years like the creation of mountain ranges such as the Alps.

temperate climate
An area of the planet where the change in temperature and rainfall between summer and winter are quite moderate and not extreme.

tourist resort
A place where people go on holiday.

UNESCO
The United Nations Educational, Scientific and Cultural Organization, whose aim is to promote goodwill amongst different countries by sharing science, education and culture.

vaccine
A way of preventing infectious diseases by introducing the body to a milder and safer form of a disease that allows the body to recognise the disease and produce antibodies to fight the dangerous version of the disease.

viaduct
A long bridge that carries railways or roads over wide gaps like valleys or gorges.

vineyards
A place where grapes are produced, usually to make wine.

BOOKS TO READ

Young Reporter in France: (series includes: Home Life, Having Fun, School Days, Special Days and Holidays) by Sue Finnie and Daniele Bourdais (Franklin Watts, 2014)

Eyewitness Travel Family Guide: France (Dorling Kindersley, 2014)

Eyewitness Travel Family Guide: Paris by Beverley Smart (Dorley Kindersley, 2014)

Lonely Planet France's Best Trips by Oliver Berry (Lonely Planet, 2013)

The Rough Guide to France by David Abram, Nikki Bayley, Ruth Blackmore (Rough Guides, 2013)

Not for Parents Paris: Everything You Wanted to Know (Lonely Planet Not for Parents) (Lonely Planet 2011)

France: Horrible Histories Special by Terry Deary and Martin Brown (Scholastic, 2011)

Looking at Countries: France by Jillian Powell (Franklin Watts, 2010)

WEBSITES

Lonely Planet's guide is a great introduction to France and tells you the best places to visit, historical, geographical and other interesting information as well as food and drink to sample and practical information about money, health, language and local customs.

www.lonelyplanet.com/france

The Rough Guide to France is packed with interesting and vital information for your visit to France. There are tips on where and when to travel, including some great itineraries to inspire your very own journey around France.

http://www.roughguides.com/destinations/europe/france/

The Michelin guide to France provides all the information you need for a great, safe journey around France. Find out the best places to visit, discover some exciting leisure activities and check out its suggested travel routes.

http://travel.michelin.com/web/destination/France

It's always best to check out official government websites before you make any journey overseas. You can find out about the latest news and information that will affect your journey to France on this UK government website.

https://www.gov.uk/foreign-travel-advice/france

Note to parents and teachers:
Every effort has been made by the Publishers to ensure that the websites in this book are suitable for children, that they are of the highest educational value, and that they contain no inappropriate or offensive material. However, because of the nature of the Internet, it is impossible to guarantee that the contents of these sites will not be altered. We strongly advise that Internet access is supervised by a responsible adult.

INDEX